To

_____

From

_____

*We dedicate this book as much to
ourselves and our children as we do to you and yours.
Oh, that we might attain to all that is written here!
Be encouraged and strengthened by Christ's love
and wisdom. He **does** know how this will all turn out.*

RON & CAESAR

The Heart
of a Father

By Ron DiCianni

Compiled by Caesar Kalinowski

Tyndale House Publishers
WHEATON, ILLINOIS

Visit Tyndale's exciting Web site at www.tyndale.com

For more information on this image or any of Ron's work, please call 800-391-1136 or visit us on-line at www.art2see.com

Designed by Melinda Schumacher

Scripture quotations marked KJV are taken from the *Holy Bible*, King James Version.

Scripture quotations marked NASB are taken from the *New American Standard Bible*, copyright © 1960, 1962, 1963, 1968, 1971, 1972, 1973, 1975, 1977 by The Lockman Foundation. Used by permission.

Scripture quotations marked NIV are taken from the *Holy Bible*, New International Version ®. NIV ®. Copyright © 1973, 1978, 1984 by International Bible Society. Used by permission of Zondervan Publishing House. All rights reserved.

Scripture quotations marked NLT are taken from the *Holy Bible*, New Living Translation, copyright © 1996. Used by permission of Tyndale House Publishers, Inc., Wheaton, Illinois 60189. All rights reserved.

Scripture quotations marked TLB are taken from the *The Living Bible* copyright © 1971. Used by permission of Tyndale House Publishers, Inc., Wheaton, Illinois 60189. All rights reserved

ISBN 0-8423-3421-1

Printed in Italy

07 06 05 04 03 02 01
7   6   5   4   3   2   1

PRIVILEGE OF PARENTS

❧

"There is no greater privilege
than to indelibly impact the life of a child for Christ.
There is also nothing so challenging."

Ron DiCianni

Begin very early to instruct a child on the true values of life. Love for all mankind. Kindness. Integrity. Trustworthiness. Truthfulness. And devotion to God.

—Dr. James Dobson

Rules for a Godly Home Life:
Let your life be modest and reserved,
your manner courteous,
your admonitions friendly,
your forgiveness willing,
your promises true,
your speech wise, and share gladly in
the bounties you receive.

—Unknown

When the Holy Spirit controls our lives, he will produce this kind of fruit in us: love, joy, peace, patience, kindness, goodness, faithfulness, gentleness, and self-control.

—Galatians 5:22-23, nlt

*I*magine how it would affect our children's attitudes and behaviors if they really believed that every breath they drew, every morsel they ate, every muscle they moved, every pleasure they experienced, was a gift from a powerful and loving God. Imagine the reverence, the dependence on God such an attitude would produce!

—JOSH MCDOWELL

*P*ursue faith and love and peace, and enjoy the companionship of those who call on the Lord with pure hearts.

—2 TIMOTHY 2:22, NLT

Happy the home when God is there,
And love fills every breast;
When one their wish, and one their prayer,
And one their heavenly rest.

—HENRY WARE, JR.

"And they shall be My people, and I will be
their God; and I will give them one heart and one
way, that they may fear Me always, for their own
good, and for the good of their children after
them."

—JEREMIAH 32:38-39, NASB

If we believe what the Bible says about love being the "greatest of them all," we will make loving God, our families, and one another the top priority in our lives.

—UNKNOWN

It is in the home that the child learns the basic principle of accountability for actions: first to those around him, and ultimately to God.

—MAXINE HANCOCK

From everlasting to everlasting the Lord's love is with those who fear him, and his righteousness with their children's children—with those who keep his covenant and remember to obey his precepts.

—Psalm 103:17-18, NIV

It's impossible for men to stress enough the importance of an older person's love and what it does to the self-image and confidence of a precious little one who feels completely approved of, unconditionally loved, and pampered just a little. Who of us wouldn't enjoy some of that once in a while? Children are a gift from God and need lots of tender, loving care.

—Chuck Snyder

From the moment our children arrive in our lives, they look to us to "mirror" information back to them about who they are. The accuracy of our reflections depends a great deal on our ability to see them clearly, as separate and unique individuals entrusted to us by God for nurturing and protection until they reach adulthood.

—Debra Evans

The Christian life is full of many balances and tensions. But the call to let Jesus Christ have His way in the hearts and lives of our children must stand above our hopes for our offspring's comfort and security. Life is a holy training ground where many hurdles and tumbles are disguised blessings if only we will let them be.

—Tony Evans

Children must come first. Your success as a family, our success as a society, depends not on what happens at the White House, but on what happens inside your house.

—Barbara Bush

The house of the righteous stands firm.

—Proverbs 12:7, niv

My father shared these character-shaping words during my childhood: "Whatever you put your mind to," he used to tell me, "you can do. And whatever you do in life—it doesn't matter if it's cleaning toilets—do it well. Do it with excellence."

—CHARLES COLSON

*L*et love and faithfulness never leave you; bind them around your neck, write them on the tablet of your heart. Then you will win favor and a good name in the sight of God and man.

—PROVERBS 3:3-4, NIV

No load too

A little boy was helping his dad move some books out of the attic into a larger room downstairs. It was important to this young boy that he was helping, even though he was probably getting in the way and slowing things down.

But the boy had a wise and patient father who knew it was more important to work at a task with his son than it was to move a pile of books efficiently. Among the books, however, were some rather large study books, and it was a chore for the boy to get them down the stairs.

On one particular trip, the boy dropped his pile of books several times. Finally, he sat down on the stairs and cried in frustration. He wasn't doing any good at all. He wasn't strong enough to carry the heavy books down the narrow stairway. It hurt him to think he couldn't do this for his daddy.

heavy

Without a word, however, the father picked up the dropped load of books, put them into the boy's arms, and scooped up both the boy and the books and carried them down the stairs.

And so they continued for load after load, both enjoying each other's company very much—the boy carrying the books and the dad carrying the boy.

—Author Unknown
Touched by an E-mail for Mothers
Edited by Denny Mog

Love never gives up,
never loses faith, is always hopeful,
and endures through every
circumstance.

— 1 Corinthians 13:7, NLT

My parents' formula was really simple:
Love the Lord consistently, love His Word,
love each other purely and devotedly,
love your children enough to both encourage
and discipline them, and teach them to love
the great resources that can make them wise.
And my parents lived out that love visibly.

—John F. MacArthur, Jr.

$\mathscr{S}$PIRITUAL $\mathbf{W}$ARFARE

"The battle for the lives and souls of our children does not lessen as they grow in faith. If anything, it intensifies. All the more reason to saturate them with the ultimate covering of a parent's prayer."

Ron DiCianni

Let us arm ourselves against our spiritual enemies with courage. They think twice about engaging with one who fights boldly.

—John Climacus

It takes faith to believe that God actually wants us to take part in His ongoing spiritual warfare and to participate in the accomplishment of His purpose.

—George Appleton

"I will give you the keys of the kingdom of heaven; whatever you bind on earth will be bound in heaven, and whatever you loose on earth will be loosed in heaven."

—Matthew 16:19, niv

Fight the good fight with all thy might!
Christ is thy strength, and Christ thy right.
Lay hold on life, and it shall be
Thy joy and crown eternally.

—John Samuel Bewley Monsell

Use every piece of God's armor to resist the
enemy in the time of evil, so that after the battle
you will still be standing firm. Stand your
ground, putting on the sturdy belt of truth and
the body armor of God's righteousness.

—Ephesians 6:13-14, NLT

If you are a Christian, you are now the sworn foe
of the legions of hell. Have no delusions about
their reality or their hostility. But do not fear them.
The God inside you terrifies them.
They cannot touch you, let alone hurt you.
But they can still seduce and they will try.
They will also oppose you as you obey Christ.
If you are serious about Christ being your Lord and
God, you can expect opposition. But life with Jesus
can be an exhilarating and reassuring experience
of constant triumph over evil forces.

—JOHN WHITE

❧

Each one of you will put to flight a thousand of
the enemy, for the Lord your God fights for you,
just as he has promised.

—JOSHUA 23:10, NLT

Jesus! the name high over all,
In hell or earth or sky;
Angels and men before it fall,
And devils fear and fly.

—Charles Wesley

God is stronger than fire and destruction, and even in the valleys of deepest darkness, rod and staff are put into our hands and bridges are thrown across the abyss.

—Helmut Thielicke

Yea, though I walk through the valley of the shadow of death, I will fear no evil: for thou art with me; thy rod and thy staff they comfort me.

—Psalm 23:4, KJV

God is in control. He is never surprised by events that surprise us. Neither is He worried over world conditions. We rest in Him who is Lord of all. His grace, mercy, and loving-kindness overwhelm us.

—Leslie B. Flynn

If God be for us, who can be against us? Nay, in all these things we are more than conquerors through him that loved us.

—Romans 8:31, 37, kjv

Onward, Christian soldiers,
Marching as to war,
With the cross of Jesus
Going on before.

—Sabine Baring-Gould

O God, our King,

whose sovereign sway

The glorious hosts of heaven obey,

And devils at Thy presence flee;

Blest is the man that trusts in Thee.

—Isaac Watts

As a Christian I am called to rest my faith

firmly on God and on the promises of God's word,

no matter what evil lurks around me. Jesus said that

this was the solid rock on which the house of my life

would stand firm against even the fiercest storms.

—David Watson

In this world, you will be tempted. The kinds of temptation in Satan's war against you may change: Candies for kids, sensuality for the young, riches for the middle-aged and power for the aging. The Evil One knows your Achilles' heel. But temptation itself need not dismay you. It was your Savior's lot and it will be yours. The Enemy seeks to destroy your fellowship with God. But as you ask God for his help, the Spirit will assist you in holding firm against that temptation.

—John White

So do not fear,
  for I am with you;
do not be dismayed,
  for I am your God.
I will strengthen you
  and help you;
I will uphold you with
  my righteous right hand.

—Isaiah 41:10, NIV

Be strong in the Lord and in his mighty power.

—Ephesians 6:10, NIV

Do not be overcome by evil, but overcome evil
with good.

—Romans 12:21, NIV

A Mighty Fortress Is Our God

A mighty fortress is our God,
A bulwark never failing;
Our helper He amid the flood
Of mortal ills prevailing.
For still our ancient foe
Doth seek to work us woe—
His craft and pow'r are great,
And, armed with cruel hate,
On earth is not His equal.

And though this world, with devils filled,
Should threaten to undo us,
We will not fear, for God hath willed
His truth to triumph through us.
The prince of darkness grim,
We tremble not for him—
For lo! his doom is sure:
One little word shall fell him.

That word above all earthly pow'rs,
No thanks to them, abideth;
The Spirit and the gifts are ours
Through Him who with us sideth.
Let goods and kindred go,
This mortal life also—
The body they may kill;
God's truth abideth still:
His kingdom is forever.

—MARTIN LUTHER

Faith...dependence on God

"God does not want to be at the top of our list of important people and things. He wants to be at the center of them all, since they all revolve around him anyway."

Ron DiCianni

Circumstances may appear to wreck our lives and God's plans, but God is not helpless among the ruins. He comes in and takes the calamity and uses it victoriously, working out his wonderful plan of love.

—ERIC LIDDELL

Your faithfulness extends to every generation, as enduring as the earth you created. Your laws remain true today, for everything serves your plans.

—PSALM 119:90-91, NLT

God holds you in the palm of His hand.

—IRISH BLESSING

Be still, my soul! the Lord is on thy side;

Bear patiently the cross of grief or pain;

Leave to thy God to order and provide;

In every change He faithful will remain.

Be still, my soul! thy best, thy heavenly Friend

Through thorny ways leads to a joyful end.

—KATHARINA AMALIA VON SCHLEGEL

I have called you by name; you are mine.
When you go through deep waters and
great trouble, I will be with you.

—ISAIAH 43:1-2, TLB

Great is your faithfulness.

—LAMENTATIONS 3:23, NIV

'Tis so sweet to trust in Jesus,
Just to take Him at His Word,
Just to rest upon His promise,
Just to know "Thus saith the Lord."
Jesus, Jesus, how I trust Him!
How I've proved Him o'er and o'er!
Jesus, Jesus, precious Jesus!
O for grace to trust Him more!

—LOUISA M. R. STEAD

Faith is not the feeling
of a moment,
but the conscious decision
for a way of life.

—MARION STROUD

Don't be anxious about tomorrow.
God will take care of your tomorrow too.
Live one day at a time.

—Matthew 6:34, TLB

Faith is the one area in our lives
where growing up means we must
grow to be more like a child,
trusting simply in the goodness and
complete knowledge of a Father who
has our best interests at heart.

—Colleen Townsend Evans

Faith is a living thing. It is like a plant that needs constant feeding. If we take daily and active steps to nourish our faith we shall find ourselves kept in God's peace and love, whatever storms may be raging around us. It is only as we spend time worshipping God, concentrating on the nature of his Person, especially his greatness and love, that our faith begins to rise.

—DAVID WATSON

Just as you received Christ Jesus as Lord, continue to live in him, rooted and built up in him, strengthened in the faith as you were taught, and overflowing with thankfulness.

—COLOSSIANS 2:6-7, NIV

My faith looks up to Thee,
*   Thou Lamb of Calvary, Savior divine!*
Now hear me while I pray, Take all my guilt away,
*   O let me from this day Be wholly Thine!*

—RAY PALMER

❦

When upon life's billows you are tempest-tossed,
When you are discouraged, thinking all is lost,
Count your many blessings—name them one by
one, And it will surprise you what the Lord hath
done.

—JOHNSON OATMAN, JR.

It is impossible to please God without faith.
Anyone who wants to come to him must believe that
there is a God and that he rewards those who
sincerely seek him.

—HEBREWS 11:6, NLT

Parental love must value maturity more than security, and it needs to know when to relax one's grasp. This letting go process brings anxiety because our human love yearns to protect and hold our loved ones close. But such security is not ours to give.

—TONY EVANS

Our God is so trustworthy that we are to throw our confidence on Him, not leaning on our own limited understanding. If God's mind was small enough for me to understand, He wouldn't be God!

—STEVE ESTES AND JONI EARECKSON TADA

For the Lord is good
and his love endures forever;
his faithfulness continues through
all generations.

—PSALM 100:5, NIV

Faith is grounded in the assurance that God accepts and uses us just as we are.

—Denise Turner

Faith is knowing God is still triumphant. Our circumstances may be challenging, but God is not wringing His hands, wondering how He is going to work things out.

—Charles R. Swindoll

I arise today through God's strength to pilot me: God's might to uphold me, God's wisdom to guide me.

—Patrick of Ireland

To give yourself up to God, to make a lifelong commitment, assumes a complete turn toward Christ as the source of strength.

—Ulrich Eggers

FAITH and obedience are bound up in the same bundle. He that obeys God trusts God; and he that trusts God obeys God. He that is without faith is without works; and he that is without works is without faith.

—Spurgeon

I can do everything with the help of Christ who gives me the strength I need.

—Philippians 4:13, nlt

PRAYER

❦

"Prayer is not a preparation for the battles of life.
It is the battle, and the battlefield is wherever we pray."

Ron DiCianni

God is the heavenly Father
who will always be there
when you seek him and find him
at the altar of prayer.

—HELEN STEINER RICE

Prayer is not you trying to move God. Prayer is among other things being caught up in God's directions and activity. He orders the affairs of the universe, and he invites you to participate by prayer. Intercession is God and you in partnership, bringing his perfect plans into being.

—JOHN WHITE

Such gracious access is granted to us even by the King of heaven, and day and night his ready hearing and his help are within the reach of all that come to him.

—DWIGHT L. MOODY

Prayer is the Christian's vital breath,
The Christian's native air,
His watchword at the gates of death;
He enters heaven with prayer.

—James Montgomery

A single grateful thought raised to heaven is the most perfect prayer.

—Gotthold Ephraim Lessing

This is the confidence we have in approaching God: that if we ask anything according to his will, he hears us. And if we know that he hears us—whatever we ask—we know that we have what we asked of him.

—1 John 5:14-15, niv

We cannot pray and remain the same. We cannot pray and have our homes remain the same. We cannot pray and have the world about us remain the same. God has decreed to act in response to prayer. "Ask," he commands us. And Satan trembles in fear we will.

—Ruth Bell Graham

Nothing flies beyond the reach of prayer except that which lies outside the will of God.

—Duncan Campbell

The Lord is near to all who call on him, to all who call on him in truth.

—Psalm 145:18, niv

If I fail to spend two hours in prayer each morning the devil gets the victory through the day. I have so much business I cannot get on without three hours daily in prayer.

—MARTIN LUTHER

God [is] the Life, the Truth, the Way;
The path of prayer Thyself hast trod:
Lord, teach us how to pray!

—JAMES MONTGOMERY

Let me hear of your unfailing love to me in the morning, for I am trusting you. Show me where to walk, for I have come to you in prayer.

—PSALM 143:8, NLT

Our Father, grant us, this day,
the sense of your presence to lift us up,
your light to direct us,
and strength for your work.

—THE ALTAR AT ROME

Prayer can leap over oceans, speed across
burning deserts, spring over mountains, bound
through jungles, and carry the healing, helping
power of the Gospel to the object of prayer. It
is a two-way conversation: it is our talking to
God and his talking to us.

—BILLY GRAHAM

Jesus told them, "I assure you, if you have
faith and don't doubt, . . . you will receive
whatever you ask for in prayer."

—MATTHEW 21:21-22, NLT

$\mathcal{W}$e have been granted the privilege of entering into intercessory prayer for our loved ones and of holding their names and faces before the Father.

—Dr. James Dobson

$\mathcal{W}$e pray . . . that you may live a life worthy of the Lord and may please him in every way: bearing fruit in every good work, growing in the knowledge of God, being strengthened with all power according to his glorious might so that you may have great endurance and patience.

—Colossians 1:10-11, niv

And now unto him who is able to keep us from falling and lift us from the dark valley of despair to the bright mountain of hope, from the midnight of desperation to the daybreak of joy; to him be power and authority, for ever and ever.

—MARTIN LUTHER KING'S PRAYER

The only real stability in our world is the Cross of Christ. So, to that Cross we turn, praying that God will give us the courage to do only what needs to be done in God's eyes, through the power of his Spirit.

—LARRY BURKETT

In the day of my trouble I will call to you, for you will answer me.

—PSALM 86:7, NIV

I urge you, first of all, to pray for all people. As you make your requests, plead for God's mercy upon them, and give thanks. Pray this way for kings and all others who are in authority, so that we can live in peace and quietness, in godliness and dignity. This is good and pleases God our Savior, for he wants everyone to be saved and to understand the truth.

— 1 Timothy 1:2-4, NLT

The highest and greatest result of praying in His name is joy whatever your circumstances.

—Joni Eareckson Tada

What a Friend we have in Jesus,
All our sins and griefs to bear!
What a privilege to carry
Everything to God in prayer!

—Joseph Medlicott Scriven

The Spirit also helpeth our infirmities: for we know not what we should pray for as we ought: but the Spirit itself maketh intercession for us with groanings which cannot be uttered.

—Romans 8:26, kjv

God my Savior, please show me your ways and teach me your paths. Help me submit my choices and decisions to you, and to let your truth guide me and teach me. In the name of Jesus Christ, I pray. Amen.

—Josh McDowell

You have taught children and nursing infants to give you praise. O Lord, our Lord, the majesty of your name fills the earth!

—Psalm 8:2, 9, nlt

The time we spend in having our daily audience with God is the most precious part of the whole day.

—Mother Teresa

I'm glad that we grew up as a family
that prayed together,
and I'm also glad that we were a family
that ate together at the dinner table.
In those days, it was normal.
Only as I see what is happening in homes
today do I realize the wisdom of this practice.
We didn't eat until everyone was at the table.
Even Mother sat down for the prayer
before eating, getting up again afterwards
to tend to the final details of the meal.

—Kenneth Taylor